56

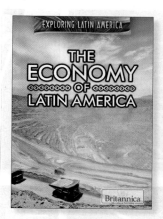

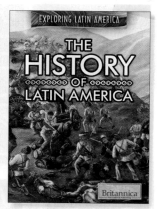

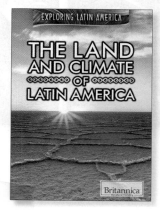

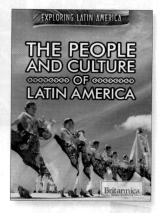

THE ECONOMY OF LATIN AMERICA

CARLA MOONEY

Britannica®
Educational Publishing

IN ASSOCIATION WITH

ROSEN
EDUCATIONAL SERVICES

Published in 2018 by Britannica Educational Publishing (a trademark of Encyclopædia Britannica, Inc.) in association with The Rosen Publishing Group, Inc.
29 East 21st Street, New York, NY 10010

Distributed exclusively by Rosen Publishing.
To see additional Britannica Educational Publishing titles, go to rosenpublishing.com.

First Edition

Britannica Educational Publishing

J.E. Luebering: Executive Director, Core Editorial
Andrea R. Field: Managing Editor, Compton's by Britannica

Rosen Publishing

Carolyn DeCarlo: Editor
Nelson Sá: Art Director
Michael Moy: Series Designer
Michael Moy: Book Layout
Cindy Reiman: Photography Manager
Karen Huang: Photo Researcher

Library of Congress Cataloging-in-Publication Data

Names: Mooney, Carla, 1970- author.
Title: The economy of Latin America / Carla Mooney.
Description: First Edition. | New York : Britannica Educational Publishing, [2018] | Series: Exploring Latin America | Includes bibliographical references and index.
Identifiers: LCCN 2016057937 | ISBN 9781680486797 (library bound : alk. paper) | ISBN 9781680486773 (pbk. : alk. paper) | ISBN 9781680486780 (6-pack : alk. paper)
Subjects: LCSH: Latin America—Economic conditions—Juvenile literature. | Economic development—Latin America—Juvenile literature.
Classification: LCC HC125 .M6146 2017 | DDC 338.98—dc23
LC record available at https://lccn.loc.gov/2016057937

Manufactured in the United States of America

Photo credits: Cover, p. 20: Martin Bernetti/AFP/Getty Images; pp. 4-5, 9, 18, 25, 32, 39 (background) f11photo/shutterstock.com; p.4 Getty Research Institute/Science Source; pp. 5, 11 Encyclopaedia Britannica, Inc.; p. 7 Christopher Corr/Ikon Images/Getty Images; p. 10 Cultura RM Exclusive/Philip Lee Harvey/Getty Images, pp. 14-15 Stockbyte/Thinkstock; p. 16 Robert Harding Picture Library; p. 19 © Andrey Plotnikov/Fotolia/Encyclopaedia Britannica; p. 21, 30, 40 Bloomberg/Getty Images; p. 22 Pav Jordan/Reuters/Newscom; p. 26 Jo Kearney/Corbis Documentary/Getty Images; p. 27 John Seaton Callahan/Moment/Getty Images; p. 28-29 Joe Raedle/Hulton Archive/Getty Images; p. 33 Grant Ordelheide/Getty Images; pp. 34-35 Venturelli Luca/Shutterstock.com; p. 36 The Asahi Shimbun/Getty Images; p. 41 cokada/E+/Getty Images; p. 43 Robert Daemmrich Photography Inc./Sygma/Getty Images; back cover By Filipe Frazao/Shutterstock.com.

CONTENTS

INTRODUCTION   **4**

CHAPTER ONE
AGRICULTURE, FISHING, AND FORESTRY   **9**

CHAPTER TWO
NATURAL RESOURCES   **18**

CHAPTER THREE
MANUFACTURED GOODS   **25**

CHAPTER FOUR
TOURISM AND SERVICES   **32**

CHAPTER FIVE
ECONOMIC FUTURE   **39**

GLOSSARY   **45**

FOR FURTHER READING   **46**

INDEX   **47**

INTRODUCTION

The region of Latin America covers all the Americas south of the US border—Mexico, Central America, South America, and the West Indies—about 15 percent of the earth. Its diverse land includes rain forest, desert, and savanna. The largest countries in Latin America by area are Brazil, Argentina, Mexico, Peru, Colombia, Bolivia, Venezuela, and Chile. Historically, their economies have traditionally been driven by the production of commodities such as oil, silver, and corn. In more recent years, growth in services and manufacturing have played a larger part in their markets overall.

From the late fifteenth through the eighteenth centuries, Portugal and Spain controlled most of mainland Latin America. Spain, the Netherlands, Britain, and France controlled various Caribbean islands. In the early nineteenth century, independence movements swept through most of Latin America. Today, most Latin American countries are independent nations, although some West Indian islands remain part of European nations.

A Spanish map from the sixteenth century shows the region that is modern-day Mexico. Most of Latin America was ruled by Spain or Portugal.

Latin America stretches from Mexico in the north to the tip
of South America, including all of the countries that make up
Central America, South America, and the West Indies.

After gaining their independence, many Latin American countries set up republics. They modeled these governments after governments in northern Europe and the United States. Many countries experienced political instability. National governments were rapidly replaced. This political instability also affected the region's economies. The countries struggled to find sources of income to pay for new military and government expenses. The governments commonly found themselves in financial difficulties.

In the nineteenth century, industrialization spread through Europe and North America. These countries turned to Latin America for its raw materials. By the second half of the nineteenth century, Latin America became an important exporter of raw materials. Most Latin American countries had one or two main exports—typically minerals or foods—until the 1950s. Relying on only a few exports made these countries vulnerable to changes in global demand.

Although many people talk about Latin America as one region, there are enormous differences in the area. The people live in a large number of independent nations, and the geography and climate of each country can vary greatly. As a result, the economies of each nation are diverse. Areas such as Mexico and Central America export many manufactured goods, while countries in South America are major exporters of agricultural commodities, petroleum, and minerals such as iron ore.

Most of Latin America's economies rely on capitalism. In this type of economy, trade and industry are generally controlled by private companies. However, the governments intervene in some areas of investment, industry, land ownership, and trade.

Today, agriculture remains an important part of the Latin American economy. In general, about one-fourth of

Made up of many independent countries, Latin America is a very diverse region that is rich in natural resources. Each area has its own native plants, animals, and resources.

Latin American workers work in agriculture. In some poorer countries like Haiti and Nicaragua, the number is even higher. Services are a large and growing economic sector, while manufacturing remains important. Still, Latin America depends heavily on its exports of commodities, which makes it vulnerable to changes in market demand and world prices.

CHAPTER ONE

AGRICULTURE, FISHING, AND FORESTRY

Latin America's economy relies on the export of foods and primary goods, such as coffee from Brazil and Colombia, beef from Argentina, and bananas from Ecuador. It also benefits from rich fishing grounds in the Caribbean Sea, Atlantic Ocean, and Pacific Ocean.

AGRICULTURE AND FARMING

Many of Latin America's staple foods have been grown since ancient times, including corn, beans, and squash in Mexico and Central America; quinoa, corn, and potatoes in the Andes; and cassava and citrus fruits in lowland rain forests. Rice, plantains, and bananas are vital to the Latin American diet.

Export of raw materials and foods is a major part of the Latin American economy. Between 2012 and 2014, the region exported an estimated 16 percent of global food and agricultural products. Fertile highlands have made Brazil, Mexico, Guatemala, and Colombia some of the world's leading coffee producers. Brazil is the world's largest exporter of coffee; the country produced 2,594,100,000 kilograms of coffee beans in 2014 alone. Ecuador, Mexico, and Peru are also leading producers of cacao, the source of cocoa.

In tropical regions such as Ecuador and Brazil, farmers grow crops such as avocado, pineapple, guava, papaya, and cashews. Sugarcane and bananas are grown throughout the West Indies. In addition to crops, Latin American farmers also raise and export livestock. Brazil, Argentina, Mexico, and Uruguay send hundreds of millions of cattle, pigs, and sheep to local and foreign markets.

In hot, dry areas of Latin America, farmers grow heavily irrigated crops such as rice and

Staple foods that are grown in Peru and used in traditional Peruvian cooking. Many of Latin America's staple foods have been grown for centuries and remain an important part of local economies.

Because the wool produced by llamas is very soft and lanolin-free, it is in demand for use in high-quality textiles around the world.

cotton. In colder climates near the south of Argentina and Chile and in the Andes Mountains, thousands of native potato species and the quinoa plant grow. In addition, ranchers raise sheep, llamas, alpacas, and vicuñas in cold climates. Ranchers breed these animals for their meat and wool, which is then used to make high-quality textiles that are exported around the world.

DEFORESTATION

In the Amazon Basin and other tropical regions, people have cleared centuries-old rain forests to create more land for farming and ranching. Farmers often use a technique called slash-and-burn farming to clear the land. First, they cut down all the plants and strip the trees of bark. Once the stripped trees and plants have dried out, the farmers set them on fire. The resulting ash returns nutrients from the trees and plants to the soil. However, heavy rains often wash away the nutrients within a few years and the farmers must move on to clear new land for crops.

Ranchers also use slash-and-burn techniques to clear land for livestock. They plant grasses on the cleared land for cattle grazing. After about four years, the grasses stop growing and the ranchers are forced to move on to new land. The land left behind is often barren and unable to yield crops. The rain forest can take up to fifty years to grow back. In addition to farming and ranching, commercial logging operations cut down rain forest trees for lumber and other products.

In many cases, deforestation can have devastating consequences on the environment. Tropical rain forests hold about 50 percent of the plant and animal species on earth. Destroying their habitat can lead to some of these species becoming extinct.

In addition, deforestation can impact the climate. Because up to 30 percent of the rain that falls in the rain forest is recycled by the forest into the atmosphere, cutting down rain forest can reduce rainfall and create a dryer, hotter climate. And because plants use carbon dioxide to produce oxygen, deforestation can lead to more carbon dioxide in the atmosphere. Carbon dioxide is a greenhouse gas that can trap heat. Adding more to the atmosphere can cause changes in climate and ocean levels. For many people in Latin America, preserving and conserving forest resources has become an important priority.

FORESTRY AND FISHING

In the tropical regions of Latin America, forestry plays a valuable part in the economy. Forestry is the practice of managing and using the natural resources of trees and other forest vegetation. Many tree species such as mahogany and rosewood grow in the rain forests near the Amazon River basin. These trees are cut down and exported to foreign countries. Manufacturers use the wood to make wood cabinets, floors, and furniture. In some countries such as Chile, entire tree plantations grow trees. They process the trees into wood chips, plywood, and paper pulp for exporting.

Lower-grade tree wood is an important part of the Latin American construction market. Eucalyptus trees grow

Thick smoke covers the rain forest as farmers use slash-and-burn methods to set fire to the trees and plants in the forest and prepare the land for growing crops.

quickly and can be used as a low-cost building material. Many Latin American communities also use eucalyptus wood as a fuel.

The waters off Peru, Chile, and Ecuador are some of the world's best fishing grounds. The cold Peru Current flows north along the Pacific Coast from southern Chile to the Equator. The cold current causes upwelling of deep ocean water and brings nutrients close to the water's surface. Along with sunlight, these nutrients allow rich plankton to grow. The nutrient-rich waters are home to a variety of fish species, from whales to shrimp. For this reason, many Latin American countries along the Pacific Coast rely on fishing. Chile is a leading producer of farm-raised salmon and trout. Ecuador is an important world exporter of shrimp. In Peru and Chile, anchovies are processed into fishmeal, which is then used in animal feed and fertilizer.

Fishermen haul in a load of anchovies off the coast of Peru. Many Latin American countries that border the Pacific Ocean rely on its rich fishing grounds as part of their economies.

A RISKY POSITION

For some parts of Latin America, a large portion of the economy depends upon the export of only a handful of products. For these countries, this dependence can be risky. Natural disasters such as hurricanes, droughts, or floods can ruin the season's crops and cause great economic hardship to the people. In addition, changes in world demand and prices can also affect the local economies. When demand and prices increase, the economy thrives and grows. However, if world demand or prices fall, the region's economy often suffers.

CHAPTER TWO

NATURAL RESOURCES

Latin America is a region rich in natural resources. Enormous supplies of oil and natural gas lie beneath the land and coastal waters of Brazil, Mexico, and Venezuela. Bolivia, Argentina, Trinidad and Tobago, and Colombia have large supplies of natural gas. Valuable metals such as gold, silver, copper, and iron ore are found in Mexico, Peru, Brazil, Chile, and other countries. From iron and gold to petroleum and natural gas, Latin America's natural resources are an important part of the region's economy.

MINING METALS

The mining industry is one of Latin America's most important economic activities. Latin America's territory covers approximately one-sixth of the Earth. It produces much of the world's three most important metals: iron ore, copper, and gold.

Latin America holds about one-fifth of the world's reserves of iron ore. Iron ore is a rock or mineral that can be heated and used to extract the metal iron. Iron ore is typically found in the form of the iron oxides magnetite and hematite. These are chemical compounds that combine iron and oxygen. The iron and steel industries worldwide rely on iron ore as a raw material. Most iron ore is used to make pig iron, a raw material in steel. The steel produced is used to make cars, trains, ships, construction beams, furniture, paper clips, tools, bicycles, and thousands of other products.

With its vast iron ore deposits, Brazil is the world's third largest producer of iron ore. In 2015 Brazil produced 428 million metric tons of iron ore. The Carajas mine in

Magnetite is an iron ore with magnetic properties. It is also known as lodestone. Several Latin American countries mine magnetite and other iron ores for export to the iron and steel industries worldwide.

northern Brazil is one of the world's largest iron ore mines. The Carajas mine produces about 300,000 metric tons of iron ore each day.

Along with iron ore, Latin America is a leading producer of copper. Because it is a good conductor of heat and resists corrosion, copper is a metal that is used around the world in electrical wiring and equipment. More than 25 percent of the world's known copper reserves are located in Latin America, mostly in Chile and Peru. Chile is the world's largest copper producer, producing 5.7 million metric tons in 2015. In northern Chile, the Chuquicamata mine is the world's largest open-pit copper mine. It measures 2.7 miles (4.3 kilometers) long, 1.8 mi (3 km) wide and more than 2,780 feet (847 meters) deep. The mine produces more

Several large lorries arrive at the Chuquicamata copper mine in the desert town of Calama, Chile. The mine is the largest open-pit copper mine in the world.

than 25 percent of Chile's copper. Peruvian mines produced 1.6 million metric tons of copper in 2015, making Peru the world's third largest copper producer, behind only Chile and China.

Latin America also mines and exports gold. Gold is a precious metal that is in high demand around the world for its use in jewelry. Buyers also purchase gold as a way to protect wealth and manage risk in financial portfolios. In addition, some technologies use gold in their design. Gold is a highly conductive and malleable metal. These properties allow gold to conduct signals effectively across the chip wiring inside smartphones. Latin America, particularly through mines in Peru and Mexico, produces approximately 17 percent of the world's gold.

Latin America's gold exports are used in the chip wiring inside smartphones. Because gold is a conductive metal, it effectively transfers signals across the smartphone motherboard.

MINING'S ENVIRONMENTAL DAMAGE

In Latin America, mining operations have damaged the environment. Metal mining can cause erosion and sedimentation and can contaminate waters and rivers with chemicals and other toxic agents. In addition, mine drainage and cooling produce large amounts of polluted water which can contaminate local drinking water and harm agricultural and farming lands. In some areas, mining projects cause deforestation, which destroys local ecosystems, plants, and wildlife.

The El Toro II glacier straddles Chile and Argentina. Evidence shows the glacier has been damaged and is shrinking due to water contamination caused by a nearby open-pit mine.

On the Argentine-Chilean border, the Pascua Lama open-pit mine is located near the San Guillermo Biosphere Reserve and a water reserve with glaciers. Evidence shows that three glaciers have been damaged by underground water contamination. The damage has led to the glaciers shrinking, which affects water supplies in the dry Atacama Desert.

At a gold mine in Panama, workers cut down acres of forest and vegetation to clear land for roads, heliports, camps, and processing plants. In many rural communities throughout Latin America, air, water, and land pollution from local mines have destroyed the traditional natural resources on which they rely.

Other important metal deposits in Latin America include tin, which is often used to coat other metals; lead, which is used in construction, batteries, and bullets; and zinc, an anti-corrosive agent. Tin is primarily found in Brazil, Peru and Bolivia, while lead and zinc deposits are located in Peru, Bolivia, southern Brazil, and northern Argentina.

DRILLING FOR OIL AND NATURAL GAS

Some regions of Latin America have rich deposits of oil and natural gas, which are drilled for energy and fuel. Latin American oil production is mainly centered in Brazil,

Venezuela, and Mexico. Together, these countries provided 75 percent of Latin America's oil production in 2015. Globally, these countries were the world's ninth, eleventh, and twelfth largest oil producers, respectively.

Brazil has huge offshore reserves of petroleum and natural gas, notably in the southeast. Some of its offshore oil rigs operate in extremely deep water. In Venezuela, oil and gas extraction is the country's main industry. It accounts for approximately one-third of Venezuela's total gross domestic product (GDP), a measure of the amount of wealth produced in a country. Major deposits of oil and gas are found near Lake Maracaibo and the country's El Tigre region. In 2015 Venezuela produced nearly 2.7 million barrels of oil per day. As of 2015, the country has proven oil reserves of nearly 298 billion barrels, which are the biggest reserves in the world, even surpassing reserves in Saudi Arabia (268 billion barrels) and Canada (172 billion barrels). In Venezuela, the state-owned company Petroleos de Venezuela SA dominates the oil industry. Mexico also ranks among the world's leading petroleum producers. Petroleum sales account for more than a third of the federal government's revenues and a significant portion of the country's foreign-exchange earnings. The great majority of Mexico's oil exports go to the United States.

CHAPTER THREE

MANUFACTURED GOODS

Most of Latin America's countries are developing, which means that they are working towards using more technology and manufacturing. Several factors have limited industry in Latin America. In some areas such as the Andes Mountains and the Amazon rain forest, the physical geography makes it difficult to reach natural resources. In addition, the political instability of many areas has limited the number of foreign and domestic investors willing to make an investment in Latin American industry.

MANUFACTURING CENTERS

Some areas have overcome these challenges through the establishment of manufacturing centers. Often, the countries that have been able to industrialize have reported higher numbers of skilled workers, good energy sources, transportation networks, and plentiful natural resources. Mexico, Brazil, and Argentina produce more than 80 percent of Latin America's manufactured goods. Mexico is a leading producer of motor vehicles, processed foods, and textiles. Brazil is a leading producer of steel products, cars, airplanes, textiles, and electrical goods. Argentina produces cars and processed meats.

Most factories are concentrated in major metropolitan areas such as São Paulo (in Brazil) and Mexico City. In addition, there are many assembly plants called *maquiladoras* near the border between Mexico and the United States. Other manufacturing regions include Monterrey, Mexico; Caracas, Venezuela; and Buenos Aires, Argentina. These areas produce metal goods, automobiles, machinery, electronics, and other goods. In addition to the major manufacturing centers, many medium-sized cities have factories for food products, cement, paper products, and chemicals.

Other countries in Latin America are also developing industries of their own. Puerto Rico provides chemical and pharmaceutical products, while Peru exports wool sweaters. In Venezuela, processing plants refine oil. In Costa Rica, Chile, and Nicaragua, factories produce processed foods and textiles, while the Caribbean nations of Barbados, Cuba, and Saint Kitts and Nevis refine sugar.

In Cuba, a sugar cane factory emits clouds of black smoke from its chimneys as it processes sugar cane plants and refines them into sugar for export.

URBAN SLUMS

Latin America's economic progress over the last half-century has triggered exponential growth across its major cities. However, an unintended effect of this rapid growth has been increased inefficiency in transportation, pollution, and unregulated residential population in its major cities. As Latin American workers move to cities in search of factory work, some cannot find a job or a decent place to live. Some are forced to live in crowded slums on the edges of the city. According to a 2015 report, about 113 million people in Latin America—nearly one in five—live in the sprawling slums. Shacks built with bricks, scrap metal, and wood are often perched on a vulnerable hillside or wetland. Mudslides and floods can quickly destroy entire towns. Most slums lack basic sanitation such as running water and underground sewage systems. In unsanitary conditions, disease often spreads quickly.

In Rio de Janeiro, Brazil, a crowded settlement on a hillside houses workers who labor in the city's factories.

Workers make decorative tassels for curtains in a *maquila* in Ciudad Juarez, Mexico. These manufacturing plants, often owned by foreign companies, are known as *maquiladoras* and produce goods for export.

MAQUILADORAS

In the twentieth century, American and Japanese companies built manufacturing plants in Latin America. Known as maquiladoras, these factories are primarily located along the United States-Mexico border. The arrangement benefits both the companies and the host countries. The foreign companies hire Mexican workers often at a lower wage than they could pay workers in the United States. Mexico and other host Latin American countries gain jobs and investment income. Many companies favor Mexico as a place to build factories because it is close to American and Canadian markets, has a large, young labor force, high productivity per hour, low wages, and a number of free trade agreements that favor production and exports.

Critics of the maquiladoras insist that the factories often ignore labor laws, encouraging low-paying jobs and dangerous workplaces. They also argue that the factories do not follow environmental protection laws and often pollute and damage their surrounding environment.

MEXICO'S AUTOMOBILE INDUSTRY

One of the driving factors behind Mexico's manufacturing growth is the automotive industry. Since 2004, Mexico's production of automobiles has more than doubled from 1.4 million vehicles to 3.2 million vehicles in 2014.

A production plant in Puebla, Mexico, uses robotic arms to assemble the Volkswagen AG Tiguan compact sport utility vehicle. Automobile production has increased in Mexico in recent years.

The growth is expected to continue as many automakers, including General Motors, Ford, Toyota, Honda, Volkswagen, Audi, BMW, Hyundai, and Mazda, intend to add new plants, capacity, and jobs in Mexico. Forecasts predict that new automotive plants will add another one to two million vehicles per year to Mexico's production totals. It is expected that by 2020 one of every four vehicles produced in North America will be built in Mexico.

Mexico's strong trade agreements with forty-five countries around the world have helped establish it as a good place for manufacturing and exports to Europe, South America, and North America.

CHAPTER FOUR

TOURISM AND SERVICES

The service industries are a growing part of the Latin American economy. Workers in service industries do not provide actual goods. Instead they perform actions. Teachers, car mechanics, barbers, housepainters, bankers, and domestic workers are all in service industries. In Latin America, finance, tourism, health care, education, and government are among the main activities of the economy's service sector.

TRAVEL AND TOURISM

Latin America is home to many of the world's most spectacular destinations. Travelers can explore tropical jungles, grassland steppes, barren deserts, and enormous snowy mountain peaks. The region also boasts a variety of wildlife from exotic birds to big cats. Nature lovers can relax on the beautiful beaches and explore rain forests, while adventurers trek through the Amazon or hike to the ancient Machu Picchu citadel. History seekers can explore Mayan ruins and colonial towns.

The massive Iguazu Falls located on the border of Argentina and Brazil is one of the many natural wonders that attract tourists from all over the world to Latin America.

Tourism is a big part of the economy for many countries in Latin America. According to the World Travel and Tourism Council, travel and tourism accounted for 9.2 percent of Latin America's total GDP in 2014 and is expected to rise in coming years. For many Latin American countries, tourism is the primary source of income. Tourists spend money in hotels and restaurants. They take tours of local attractions and shop in local markets. Many industries benefit from tourism, including hotels, travel agencies, airlines and other transportation services, restaurants, tour guides, and leisure activity companies.

Many international tourists flock to Latin American vacation spots. Mexico is ranked as one of the world's top ten tourist destinations, receiving 29.1 million international tourists in 2014. Brazil, Argentina, the Dominican Republic, Chile, Puerto Rico, Peru, Cuba, Uruguay, and Columbia are also popular tourist destinations.

Interestingly enough, regional travelers have an even bigger part to play in Latin America's travel and tourism industry. According to the World Tourism Organization, about 80 percent of the tourist travels made in Latin America begin and end within region—with Latin Americans traveling *within* their own countries or visiting neighboring ones. Recent improvements in infrastructure and simplification of travel between nations has certainly increased regional travel. For example, heavy investment in roads in Ecuador has opened up new areas of the country and reduced travel times. As a result, it is much easier for a person from Colombia or Peru to drive to Ecuador

Tourists explore a pyramid in Chichen Itza, a popular tourist destination in Mexico. Both regional and international tourists are drawn to the area because of its Mayan ruins.

2016 OLYMPICS

Rio de Janeiro in Brazil hosted the 2016 Summer Olympics. About 434,000 foreign visitors traveled to Brazil, spending hundreds of millions of dollars in local hotels, restaurants, and shops. In addition, 700,000 Brazilians traveled to Rio for the games. Some visitors stayed a few extra days in Brazil after attending Olympic events. Millions of people around the world saw Brazil on television. Brazilian tourism officials hope that the games were able to showcase Rio de Janeiro as a beautiful city between the sea and mountains. They hope that the lasting impact of the games will be an increase in tourists who choose to visit Latin America.

Spectators cheer as the world's best athletes parade into Maracana Stadium in Rio de Janeiro, Brazil, for the opening ceremony of the 2016 Summer Olympic Games.

for a short vacation. In addition, some Latin American countries have reduced visa requirements for their citizens, making it much easier to travel within Latin America.

INDIRECT BENEFITS OF TOURISM

When tourism is strong, businesses and industries that support the tourism industry also benefit. Construction companies earn more money when they are hired to build new hotels or transportation systems. Restaurant suppliers benefit when restaurants order more dishes or refrigerators. Textile companies benefit when hotels order more towels for their guests. In addition, government spending in areas such as visitor information services, tourism promotion, and other public services also supports the economy and creates jobs.

In popular tourist destinations, hotels, restaurants, and tour guide companies are a major source of jobs. According to the World Travel and Tourism Council, travel and tourism directly supported 6,361,000 jobs in Latin America in 2014. Including jobs created indirectly, travel and tourism supported more than 17.6 million jobs in 2014.

OTHER SERVICE INDUSTRIES

Other service industries in Latin America include banks, government agencies, and private offices. These businesses often employ large numbers of clerks. In addition, many middle-class households in Latin America employ live-in maids. According to the International Labor Organization, there are nearly 20 million domestic workers in Latin America. This number is five times more than in Western Europe and North America combined. Most of Latin America's domestic workers are women. One in every four women working in the region is a domestic worker. Most of these women are young and from low-income families.

Many service workers in Latin America are part of the "informal economy," which is also called the underground, shadow, or black market economy. Some are sidewalk vendors (of food, drinks, candies, etc.), day laborers for farms and construction sites, maids, gardeners, and even car mechanics. Black market activity also includes the illegal drug trade, which, unfortunately, remains a major source of disruption in certain Latin American countries such as Mexico and Colombia despite international efforts to stop it.

ECONOMIC FUTURE

I n the first decade of the twenty-first century, Latin America enjoyed solid economic growth. Poverty declined, while the middle class grew. However, these gains were not evenly spread across all areas. South America and Mexico are enjoying more gains thus far than Central America and the Caribbean. Latin America's economic future will depend on its ability to reduce its reliance on key commodity exports and diversify its products and industries.

REDUCING COMMODITY DEPENDENCE

Over the years, large parts of Latin America's economy have depended on commodity exports. A commodity is a basic good that is interchangeable with other goods. Commodities are typically used as raw material inputs in the production of other goods or services. Common examples of commodities are oil, natural gas, gold, grains, and beef. A country or region is considered commodity-dependent if its exports of commodities make up at least 60 percent of total exports.

In the early 2000s, commodity prices increased world-wide. Many countries in Latin America benefitted from being able to sell their commodities at higher prices. Much of this increase was driven by increasing energy and metal prices, which tripled between 2003 and 2011. During this time, China steadily increased demand for food, metals, and fuel to feed its growing industries. Responding to China's rising demand, Latin America's exports to China increased twenty-five-fold between 2000 and 2013, reaching nearly $100 billion a year. Today, China is Latin America's second largest export market, only behind the United States. Brazil is China's largest trading partner in Latin America, with Brazil

A cargo ship filled with containers arrives at the port of Veracruz, Mexico. Mexico's economic growth has slowed in recent years, with reduced demand for some manufactured goods and oil.

INCOME INEQUALITY

Most countries in Latin America have earnings far below those in more developed countries. For example, average incomes in the United States are at least six times higher than those of Argentines and Mexicans, which are, in turn, ten times higher than the incomes of Haitians and Nicaraguans. Moreover, great disparities of wealth mar societies from within. The rich are distanced from the poor though they live side by side.

Although Latin America has been able to reduce poverty in recent years, there is still a significant gap between the wealthiest residents and the poor. Latin America remains one of the most unequal regions in the world. In 2014, the richest 10 percent of citizens in Latin America held 71 percent of the region's wealth. From 2002 to 2015, Latin America's billionaires increased their wealth by an average of 21 percent annually. Although the region as a whole enjoyed economic growth, only a small number of wealthy individuals truly benefitted from it.

As shown in this aerial view of Rio de Janeiro, the city's wealthy live in modern high-rise buildings, while the poor live nearby in crowded slums.

exporting iron ore and soybeans. Argentina, Venezuela, Chile, and Peru also export soybeans, oil, copper, and fish-meal to China.

However, as demand from China began to slow in 2014, the Latin American countries that had grown reliant upon exports to China also experienced a slowdown in their economies. As commodity prices and demand from China decreased, these regions suffered a decline in exports and prices. South America, as a continent, suffered a 21 percent drop in exports in 2015—the third straight year in decline. Mexico and several Central American countries that had decreased their dependence on commodity exports were much less affected. If Latin America is unable to reduce its dependence on commodity exports going forward, it will continue to be bonded to the effects of world demand and pricing in the future.

TRADE AGREEMENTS

Some Latin American countries have entered into trade agreements with the United States and other countries. A trade agreement is agreement between at least two countries to reduce trade barriers such as import quotas and tariffs. The goal of the agreement is to increase trade of goods and services among the countries.

In 1992, Mexico, the United States, and Canada signed the North American Free Trade Agreement (NAFTA). NAFTA gradually eliminated most tariffs and other trade barriers on goods and services passing between the United States, Mexico, and Canada. The pact effectively created a free-trade bloc among the three largest countries of North America.

Demonstrators in Austin, Texas, protest the North American Free Trade Agreement (NAFTA), which eliminated most tariffs and trade barriers between the United States, Mexico, and Canada.

While NAFTA has generated economic growth for all three countries involved, it has also received some criticism. The agreement did not put environmental regulations in place. Some US companies have moved their operations to Mexico to take advantage of cheaper wages and less environmental regulation, which has created environmental problems in Mexico. In addition, NAFTA caused a loss of jobs in the United States in some sectors, though little happened in the labor market that dramatically changed the outcomes for any country involved in the treaty.

Although NAFTA failed to deliver all that its proponents had promised, it continued to remain in effect. In 2004 the Central America Free Trade Agreement (CAFTA) expanded NAFTA to include five Central American countries (El Salvador, Guatemala, Honduras, Costa Rica, and Nicaragua). In the same year, the Dominican Republic joined the group by signing a free trade agreement with the United States, followed by Colombia in 2006, Peru in 2007, and Panama in 2011. Future trade agreements may reduce trade barriers for other Latin American countries. With an easier flow of goods and services, the Latin American region would have the potential to further diversify its exports and products.

GLOSSARY

agriculture The science or occupation of farming.

capitalism A way of organizing an economy so that most forms of property and production are owned by individuals or companies rather than by the government.

climate The usual weather conditions in a particular region.

commodity Something that is bought and sold.

deforestation The act or result of cutting down or burning all the trees in an area.

economy The process by which goods and services are produced, sold, and bought in a country or region.

export To send a product to be sold in another country.

gross domestic product (GDP) The total value of the goods and services produced by a nation during a year, not including income earned in foreign countries.

industry The process of making products by using machinery and factories.

infrastructure The basic equipment and structures needed for a country, region, or organization to function properly.

instability The state of being likely to change.

producer Someone or something that grows or makes particular goods or products.

quota In international trade, an official limit on the quantity or value of the goods and services that may be imported or exported over a specified period of time.

republic A country that is governed by elected representatives and a leader (such as a president).

sector A part of an economy that includes certain types of employment or enterprises.

staple A chief commodity or production of a place.

tariff A tax on goods coming into or leaving a country.

FOR FURTHER READING

Brooks, Susie. *Brazil* (Land and the People). New York, NY: Gareth Stevens, 2016.

Fabiny, Sarah. *Where Is the Amazon?* New York, NY: Grosset & Dunlap, 2016.

Foley, Erin. *Ecuador* (Cultures of the World). New York, NY: Cavendish Square Publishing, 2016.

Roumanis, Alexis. *Rainforests* (Exploring Ecosystems). New York, NY: Weigl Publishers, 2015.

Senker, Cath. *Mexico* (Land and the People). New York, NY: Gareth Stevens, 2016.

Sirota, Lyn. *South America* (The Natural World). New York, NY: Weigl Publishers, 2014.

VanVoorst, Jennifer Fretland. *The Ancient Maya* (Exploring the Ancient World). North Mankato, MN: Compass Point, 2012.

Wiseman, Blaine. *Argentina* (Exploring Countries). New York, NY: Weigl Publishers, 2015.

Wiseman, Blaine. *Columbia* (Exploring Countries). New York, NY: Weigl Publishers, 2016.

WEBSITES

Because of the changing nature of internet links, Rosen Publishing has developed an online list of websites related to the subject of this book. This site is updated regularly. Please use this link to access this list:

http://www.rosenlinks.com/ELA/economy

INDEX

A

agriculture, 6, 8, 9–11
Amazon Basin, 12, 13
Andes Mountains, 9, 11, 25
Argentina, 4, 8, 10, 11, 18, 23, 25, 26, 34, 42
automotive industry, 30–31

B

Barbados, 26
Bolivia, 4, 18, 23
Brazil, 4, 9, 10, 18, 19, 20, 23, 24, 25, 26, 34, 36, 40

C

capitalism, 6
Carajas mine, 19–20
Central America Free Trade Agreement (CAFTA), 44
Chile, 4, 11, 13, 15, 16, 18, 20, 21, 23, 26, 34, 42
Chuquicamata mine, 20
Colombia, 4, 9, 10, 18, 34, 38, 44
copper, 20–21
Costa Rica, 26, 44
Cuba, 26, 34

D

deforestation, 12–13

E

Ecuador, 9, 10, 15, 16, 34
El Tigre region, 24
exports
 agricultural, 9–11
 automobiles, , 30–31
 fishing, 15–16
 forestry, 13
 manufactured goods, 25–26
 metals, 18–23
 oil and gas, 23–24
 reducing dependence upon, 39–42
 reliance upon, 4, 8, 17

F

factories, 26, 27, 29, 30
fishing, 15–16
forestry, 13–15

G

gold, 21
Guatemala, 10, 44

I

income inequality, 41
"informal economy," 38
iron ore, 18–20

L

Lake Maracaibo, 24
Latin America
    independence for countries in, 6
    territory, 4
    under control of European
        countries, 4
lead, 23
logging, 12

M

manufacturing centers, 25–26
maquiladoras, 26, 29–30
Mexico, 4, 6, 9, 10, 18, 21, 24,
    25, 26, 29, 30–31, 33, 38,
    39, 42, 44
mining, 18–23
    environmental damage of,
        22–23

N

natural gas, drilling, 24
Nicaragua, 8, 26, 41, 44
North American Free Trade
    Agreement (NAFTA), 42–44

O

oil, drilling, 23–24

P

Pascua Lama mine, 23
Peru, 4, 10, 15, 16, 18, 20, 21,
    23, 26, 34, 42, 44

petroleum, 6, 18, 24
Puerto Rico, 26, 34

S

Saint Kitts and Nevis, 26
service industries, 37–38
slash-and-burn farming, 12
Summer Olympics, 2016, 26

T

tin, 23
Tobago, 18
travel and tourism industries,
    32–37
    indirect benefits of, 37
Trinidad, 18

U

urban slums, 27
Uruguay, 10, 34

V

Venezuela, 4, 18, 24, 26, 42

W

West Indies, 4, 10

Z

zinc, 23